Penguin Books

Michael Leunig

GOATPERSON

AND OTHER TALES

Michael Leunig was born in Melbourne in 1945.
GOATPERSON, his sixteenth book,
is a collection of pieces that have been
previously published in the Melbourne *Age*.
Some of them have also appeared in
the *Sydney Morning Herald*.

Michael Leunig
GOATPERSON
AND OTHER TALES

PENGUIN BOOKS

Penguin Books Australia Ltd
487 Maroondah Highway, PO Box 257
Ringwood, Victoria 3134, Australia
Penguin Books Ltd
Harmondsworth, Middlesex, England
Penguin Putnam Inc.
375 Hudson Street, New York, New York 10014, USA
Penguin Books Canada Limited
10 Alcorn Avenue, Toronto, Ontario, Canada M4V 3B2
Penguin Books (NZ) Ltd
Cnr Rosedale and Airborne Roads, Albany, Auckland, New Zealand
Penguin Books (South Africa) (Pty) Ltd
24 Sturdee Avenue, Rosebank, Johannesburg 2196, South Africa
Penguin Books India (P) Ltd
11, Community Centre, Panchsheel, Park New Delhi 110 017, India

First published by Penguin Books Australia Ltd 1999

3 5 7 9 10 8 6 4 2

Text and cover design by George Dale, Penguin Design Studio
Printed and bound in Australia by McPherson's Printing Group, Maryborough, Victoria

National Library of Australia
Cataloguing-in-Publication data:

Leunig, Michael, 1945– .
Goatperson and other tales.

ISBN 0 14 029140 7.

1. Australian wit and humor, Pictorial. 2. Caricatures and cartoons – Australia. I. Title.

741.5994

www.penguin.com.au

WHY DO WE DO IT ?

Nobody seems to know why we do it.

Nobody seems to even <u>ask</u> why we do it

How strange!
It's as if everybody knows <u>PRECISELY</u> why we do it and the reason is too obvious to mention —

No voice of gentle enquiry.
No bewildered cry from
the street: the sudden
shout, "Why do we do it?!"

or perhaps too vile
and shameful to
acknowledge; or too silly.
Why the silence?

Do we do it because
everybody else does it and
because we're afraid of
not doing it?
        WHY? Please!
Somebody!
WHY DO WE DO IT?

leunig

A banished angel, weary and lost in space, found a deserted world and landed on its surface.

It seemed quite an ordinary world but peaceful and beautiful enough; there were flowers and trees — there was gravity and warmth; there was light and shade.

The angel and the soul fell in love and decided to make a go of it: their friendship and their neglected world.

An angel needs a soul and a soul needs an angel — and they both need a home. They fell in love with their simple planet.

The previous inhabitants had outgrown this place. It was not enough so they fled to a world of their own making: a world constructed of objects and obsessions — of discourse and distraction — a more <u>exciting</u> and <u>INTERESTING</u> world.

The angel came upon a footprint and soon after came face to face with a lone, abandoned soul. They smiled at each other and embraced.

At night they lay on their old world in each other's arms and gazed happily at the stars. One night a great meteor blazed across the sky.

It was the exciting new world burning up and disintegrating.
"Make a wish," said the angel.
"I'm afraid it's too late," said the soul, "Let's say a prayer instead."

Leunig

Leunig

Father, how come you've got a bar code on your forehead?

Waiter, what's this large column of froth on my coffee?

What's the problem?

Well, it's ridiculous. It has no substance. It's all show. It's modern madness. I don't want it.

I'm sorry sir. We have to offer it to be competitive. Customers expect it. That's how it comes.

Just a simple little cup of coffee?

Look! Maybe you're depressed or something. Our froth is highly esteemed and sought after—it's a talking point. People are excited. What's your problem?

FABLE.

The princess danced the night away happily with all the handsome and eligible men.

At midnight the clock began to strike twelve and all the men fled from the ballroom.

The princess gathered all this footwear together and vowed to search for the owners and so find true happiness.

In the rush to escape
every one of them
dropped a glass slipper
onto the dance floor.

She travelled far and
wide trying the
slippers on all the
men in the realm.

The slippers all seemed
to fit every man
quite comfortably and
this confused her
deeply. So now what?
Where to now?

Leunig

STUFF

There is more _stuff_ in the world than ever before.

Stuff you can touch. Stuff you can think. Stuff you can use and consume. Stuff you can know with all of your senses.

The growth of stuff is out of control. It is now being created by means of an unstoppable, exponential CHAIN REACTION.

Stuff has become a major threat to freedom and happiness. It destroys nature and peace. It steals time and space. It fouls beauty.

It is relentless, virulent, invasive and addictive. Stuff makes us exhausted and mad. There is too much stuff

The following common statements can be taken VERY seriously:—

" I'm stuffed."
and,
" The world is stuffed."

Leunig

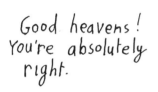
Good heavens!
You're absolutely
right.

Dingbat!

This proves what
I was saying in
the first place.

Leunig

When you throw the stale
bread to the seagulls darling....

... don't just toss it straight
into their beaks.

Try and throw it right out there into the rocks and the waves.

Make them work for it and it will improve their character!

Leunig

Keeping up with
the Joneses was
very stimulating.

Overtaking the
Joneses was very
exciting.

Watching the Joneses
come unstuck was
very satisfying.

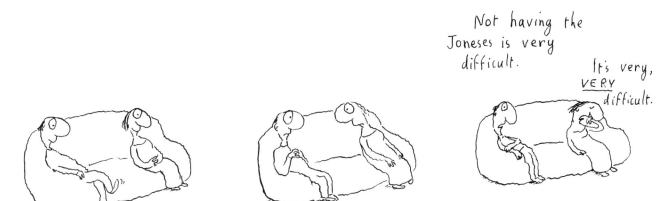

Not having the Joneses is very difficult.

It's very, VERY difficult.

Leunig

Leunig

God's grace, nature's blessings, free music from the birds — these mollycoddling handouts make us SOFT and UNCOMPETITIVE. It's time to get real and become A SELF MADE WINNER!

First you must create your own AIR and WATER; so you will need a large, reliable chemistry set and some strong STORAGE VESSELS.

Then it's just a matter of putting in the HOURS and the HARD WORK and watching the whole thing multiply.

Then you must provide your own SUNLIGHT and SOIL; and for this you will require HUGE QUANTITIES of various inflammable gases and a box of matches plus a secure LAVA supply and machinery for crushing and GRINDING.

And until you have done all of this; and until you have spurned all those subsidies from heaven: the moonlight the flowers, the sunrise etc. (which weaken us so), and until you have made it entirely ON YOUR OWN....

...YOU are not real.

Leunig

GUNK

He woke up completely covered with gunk.

All around him, everything in the room was covered with gunk.

People everywhere were smothered with it; **gunk had worked** its way into, onto EVERYTHING and EVERYONE.

And outside too, the streets,
the houses the entire city
seemed to be covered with
gunk!

How tired, heavy and dull it
made the world. Nothing sparkled
any more; nothing moved freely.

What was it? What was this
GUNK? What was it composed
of, where did it come from
and what was to be done about
it.?
Why were so many people
PROMOTING it?

leunig

CONVERT THAT WORN OUT OLD GRANDMOTHER TO CASH.

Boiled money.

What's for dinner?

The notes regurgitate easy but the coins come up all shiny from the gastric juices.

We've named her "More"

What a nice name for a girl — not like those awful old hippie names.

Let's get into bed and give each other a bit of money.

MONEY TEA

HOT WATER

DOLLAR COINS

A SOOTHING INFUSION.

What's the bedtime story tonight dad?

Five bucks up front now and another five in the morning if you go to sleep quick

AROMATHERAPY, FOOTBATH, FACIAL, etc.

$50

Leunig

If you're such a bright young thing, how come you wear so much black?

WELL, FOR A START. YOU MUST REMEMBER THAT THE OUTER PERSON IS SOMETIMES THE OPPOSITE TO THE INNER PERSON. O.K?

RIGHT.

And apart from that, I am in black because I am attending a funeral

The badly designed, embarrassing mess; the bungling boofhead; the shambling dingbat who was me is being buried...

WHO IS
BEING
BURIED ?

It is my former
self who is being
buried; the
floundering dork;
the clumsy dag
who used to be me..

Is CONSTANTLY being
buried — it's an endless
funeral. It's not easy
being the undertaker, the
priest, the grave digger
and the deceased all
at the same time!

You need to be VERY
dignified and in control —
particularly as the wretched
little basket case is always
trying to clamber out of
the hole again... in fact,
here he comes again...
the grinning fool... forgive
me, this is so embarrassing!

Leunig

GOATPERSON (special guest speaker at the GREAT writer's festival)

GOATPERSON, would you describe for us what it's like to have never written a book and what it's like to have no ambition to write.

It's just an average boring kind of feeling. It's not soulful or spiritual or anything. Just a plain, old nothing in particular situation. It's O.K.

AMAZING!!

That's just a mundane, run of the mill, nondescript feeling. Just an ordinary, shallow, empty kind of unmemorable situation. Quite unremarkable but quite O.K. ... quite o.k.

AMAZING AMAZING AMAZING AMAZING!

Goatperson, I wonder would you share with us your feelings about not making your mark or not receiving critical acclaim.... not telling your story ... not having any work which might be made into a film or a play. What could that POSSIBLY Be like : to have your soul so unacknowledged ?? Please tell us what that's like.

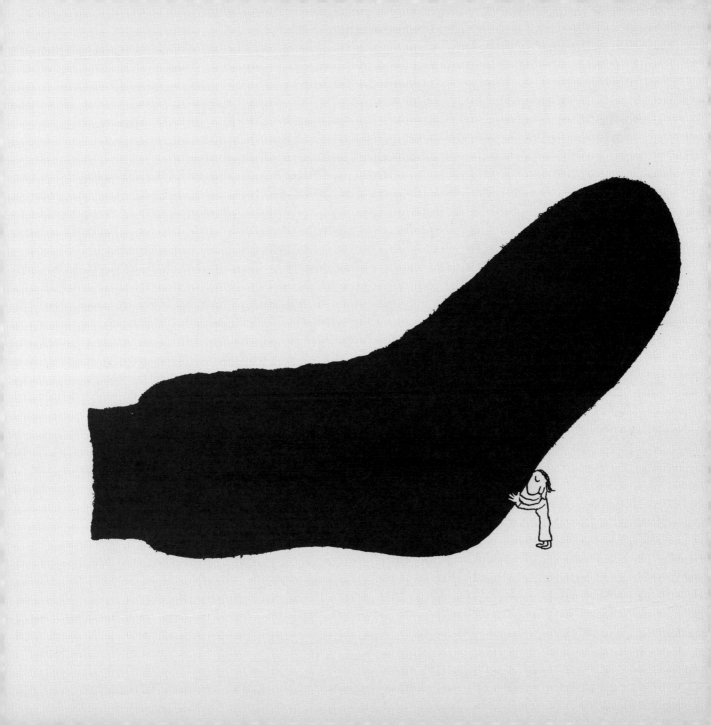

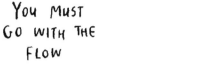

How do
I get real?

YOU MUST
GO WITH THE
FLOW

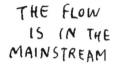

Where is
the flow?

THE FLOW
IS IN THE
MAINSTREAM

Does the
big drain
have a grille
or a grate
on it?

NO. EVERYBODY
GETS SWEPT
STRAIGHT DOWN
INTO THE
BLACK PIT.

where does
the mainstream
go?

IT GOES
DOWNWARDS
AND INTO
THE BIG DRAIN.

What is
the black
pit?

I AM REFERRING
TO THE COLD,
BLACK PIT OF
PAIN, DISINTEGRATION
AND OBLIVION.

In that case
I'd like to know
where can I buy
a nice colorful
pair of trousers
for my canary?

THIRD
FLOOR;
BIRDWEAR

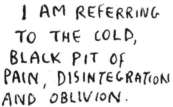

Leunig

The Summer Palace

Make a little garden in your pocket.
Plant your cuffs with radishes and rocket.
Let a passion fruit crawl up your thigh.
Grow some oregano in your fly.

Make a steamy compost of your fears.
Trickle irrigate your life with tears.
Let your troubled mind become a trellis.
Turn your heart into a summer palace

Moments of no consequence
Seem to make a lot of sense;
Like the gentle pitter patter
Of the things that do not matter
As I sit alone and stare;
Neither here and neither there.

The GOOD USES of a TIRED HUSBAND.

A door sausage to
stop the draught.

Mulch for the
rose bush.

A cushion for
the cat.

A Candlestick.

A vase.

So you can remember
where your seat is
after interval at the
concert hall.

Leunig

May your neighbor's house be perpetually renovated by a builder who loves listening to "ALL THE CLASSIC HITS FROM THE 70'S AND THE 80'S "

May your wife become greatly infatuated with the ideas of Germaine Greer.

May your favorite café become extremely fashionable

May your bottom,
somehow or other,
someday make it into
the Guinness Book of
Records

May the indicator
lever on your steering
column turn into a
pretzel.

May you develop an
ingrown toenail on a
very private part of
your body not normally
associated with ingrown
toe nails.

Leunig

Help me doctor.
I've got a book
inside me!

Most people have a
book in them. Perhaps
I can refer you to
a publisher.

You seem
<u>ashamed</u> of
<u>your</u> inner
book?

Not at all.
It's just that
I don't want to
become a.... a..

No! I don't want it published.
I want it surgically removed, —
or dissolved with herbs or something
— maybe some sort of therapy.
I WANT TO BE RID OF IT!
PLEASE!

.... I don't want to
become ——
a WRITER!

There, there — it's not so bad.
We all have to become writers
sooner or later. We must learn
acceptance. We are born,
we live and then, sadly,
we must write.

It seems so
unfair. Life is
so cruel.
I thought I
could escape.

Leunig

THE PLODDER.

You'll get left behind !

HOW WONDERFUL.

You'll miss out !

HOW LOVELY.

You won't achieve your personal best !

HOW ENJOYABLE

You won't be influential !

HOW TRUE.

You won't be attractive !
You won't be clever !

HOW DIVINE.

You won't know what's happening !

HOW PEACEFUL.

etc.

leunig

COVERED IN GUNK, HE VISITS A WISE ELDER TO DISCUSS THE MYSTERIOUS SUBSTANCE WHICH COVERS NOT ONLY HIS BODY BUT THE ENTIRE WORLD.

I feel like my whole life — my thoughts, my feelings, my actions — are covered with an invisible, numbing, clammy sludge. How can this be? What is this GUNK?

Gunk is the material which holds the modern world together. Certainly it is an encumbrance but without it our lives and our civilisations would probably fall apart. Gunk is the glue of existence!

It's like a packing material which stops everything cracking and breaking — it's a sort of shredded waste which surrounds everything and everybody and keeps things from actually touching.

There's an awful lot of it about. It seems to get worse every day. Has the world ALWAYS been covered in gunk?

Good heavens no! The world used to be held together with INNER structures and as you can tell, gunk is an external surface matter. It holds things together from the OUTSIDE

The trouble is — it's very stifling! Very gooey!

YES! I feel like I'm stewing in my own juice all the time — and everybody else's as WELL!

WELL WHAT'S IT MADE OF THIS PACKAGING MATERIAL... THIS COATING.... THIS GUNK?

Forgive me if this seems a bit crude but gunk is a mish mash blend of a million and one varieties of one hundred percent bullshit and we're all absolutely covered in it!

Leunig

Although he never actually sold his soul he buried it so deep down within himself that his feet swelled up.

So deep down that it was irretrievable: buried under the rubble of "the great lie" which he had gradually swallowed.

The great lie called "THE REAL WORLD" or "THE SYSTEM". He'd swallowed it and it was his own fault.

All that was left to remind him of his true spirit was an occasional twitching in his swollen feet where his soul was entombed

As a mark of respect he went barefoot for evermore.

"It's the real me...!" he said but nobody understood what he meant.

Leunig

Recipe for RHUBARB FOOL, an old English antidote to dark, anxious and ignominious times.

Ingredients

① Two large leaves of rhubarb.

② One longish piece of string

METHOD

① Using the piece of string, attach one rhubarb leaf to each side of head, as shown

② Stand quietly in public place for app. two hours.

Leunig

The Housewife's Guide to Sexual Happiness.

You will require firm, comfortable shoes with strong laces and soles which have a good grip.

A stout STAFF or crook is useful.

Before getting under way, tell somebody the details of your route and how long you expect to be gone.

Carry refreshments. For
example: bread, sausage, cheese
fruit and ginger ale.

A colorful beanie will
prevent heat loss through
the head and will be easy
to spot should you get into
difficulty. A whistle and
binoculars are also recommended.

It is always more pleasurable
to <u>wend</u> your way rather
than heading forcefully
toward a particular point.
Wending is a great and fine,
old art and shall be
discussed at some later date.

Leunig

Poor old lonely mother earth
Is very, very sad,
She had a bomb put in her heart
By people who were mad;
She held them and she fed them,
She taught them to be free.
They put a bomb inside her heart
And whispered, "C'est la vie"

Leunig

THE SMILE

I shot a smile into the air
It came to earth I know not where,
Perhaps on someone else's face
In some forgotten, quiet place

Perhaps somewhere a sleeping child
Has had a happy dream and smiled
Or some old soul about to die
Has smiled and made a little sigh;

Has sighed a simple, final prayer
Which lifts up gently in the air
And flows into the world, so wild,
Perhaps to wake the sleeping child.

Homes are quietly burning:
Madness on the march.
Lies move unresisted
Through the land

We stand by helpless
As our lives are occupied
Faster than we
understand.

'Alright!" You scream your
    indecision,
"Take the children — but
leave the television!"
So you stand by useless
As childhood is trashed;
Innocence reviled;
The truth is bashed

The home and the
Idea of home
Is set on fire.
And still you stand by
As the goodness in your
culture burns
You stand there in
the glow.
Going, going —
Going with the flow.

Collaborators wave
their little flags
As ugliness takes over;
"MAKE A FRIEND OF
UGLINESS" they say.
"LEARN THE LANGUAGE.
THEN YOU WON'T GET HURT

But you will —
No matter how
you crawl;
A knock on the door
one night,
A scuffle in the hall
Your heart rubbed
In the dirt

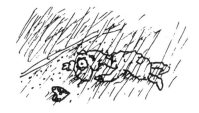

Ah yes, THE FLOW!
Heaven help us.
ONE DAY you might
Be asked, "how come
You did not know
What was going on?
Why did you not fight?"

"FIGHT?" you'll say
"that's a thought that
never occurred."
The very word
brings tears.
It will dawn on
you after all those
painful years
That to fight is one
of the most beautiful,
simple and useful ideas.

✝   leunig

I saw a goat one frosty morn
With the moon upon his horn,
With a star upon his tail,
With a bird upon his back,
With a flower upon his nose,
With his feet upon a rock,
With his eyes upon the ground,
With the frost upon his coat.
Good morning, well connected goat!

Leunig

Highlights from the 1998 FESTIVAL OF ALANS   OCT 28 — NOV 3

IT'S TIME ONCE AGAIN TO
CELEBRATE ALL MEN
NAMED ALAN.

OCT 28
THE PARADE OF ALANS

OCT 29
OPEN AIR THANKSGIVING
FOR ALAN SERVICE INCLUDING
THE BLESSING OF THE ALANS
BY THE ARCHBISHOP

OCT 30
"TAKE HOME AN ALAN DAY."

OCT 31
THE CHAIN OF ALANS.
ALANS WILL JOIN HANDS AND
CIRCLE THE CITY IN A HUMAN
CHAIN TO CREATE THE FAMOUS,
"ALAN ENERGY AURA."

NOV 1–3
THREE DAY FUN FILLED FINALE.
THE ALAN STAMPEDE RAVE
PARTY.   THREE DAYS AND
NIGHTS OF ALANS DOING THEIR
OWN THING — FREE FORMING
IT AT THE SHOWGROUNDS TO
EXPRESS "THE SPIRIT OF ALAN."

Leunig

Those people — who are they?

Those OTHER people. Those people who are not you.

Those people who are somebody else. They seem so weird and strange. What do they get up to?

What's it like to be somebody else? Look at them — they're everywhere! The others!

What do they want? Why do they exist? Look at them! Lots and lots of them but each one alone.

What do you do with people who are not you? What do you do with yourself? What do you get up to? How come?

Leunig

A SPECTACULAR EVENT
WHICH SUDDENLY SURPASSES
THE GREAT NEWS STORIES
OF THE WORLD: OUR
FATHER, NORMALLY A
WORRIED AND SERIOUS MAN,
DOES AN UNDERWATER
HANDSTAND IN THE BAY.

Here I am.
Alive on earth.
Me.

Conscious.
Unconscious.
Semi-conscious.

Knowing others.
Known to others.

Yet also unknown,
unknowable and
alone forever.

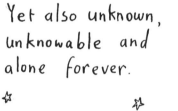

Soon I will
not be here

HURRAH !

Leunig

When you're feeling like a louse
Pop some decking on your house.

Grab a pair of yachting shoes;
Slip them on and have a cruise.

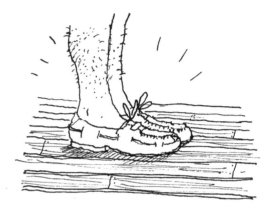

You are sailing 'round the horn;
'Round the clothes line,
'Round the lawn.

Stride across your little deck;
You are not a sunken wreck,

Danger, danger; dorsal fin
Starboard; by the wheelie bin!

Storm approaching — get below!
Time to catch the mid-day show.

Leunig

The FESTIVAL of QUIET RESIGNATION

Winter approaches. The season of FESTIVALs is almost finished. You go to one of the last: "THE FESTIVAL OF QUIET RESIGNATION"

"I might as well," you mumble to yourself.

You arrive. Nobody much has bothered to turn up but the general feeling of quiet resignation is strong. A plastic bag blows along the ground yet nobody takes any notice

It begins to rain so you walk about in the rain with quiet resignation.

The main attraction is a
mirror leaning against
a brick wall. You stand
and stare at yourself
with quiet resignation.

There is a barbecue but
the gas bottle is empty.
"C'est la vie" says the
man with quiet resignation.

As you leave you see
a member of the organising
committee sitting in a
broken plastic chair. "What
else would you expect these
days" he murmurs to
himself. "Fair enough" you
think to yourself.........
And that's it!

Leunig

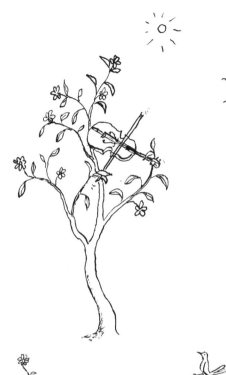

I'm looking for life's
precious little golden thread

We've got the rusty chain,
the tangled wire and
the thick rope but

I want to just SEE it
I want to SMILE at it.

we can't help
you with the golden
thread I'm afraid. What
do you want it for?

I want to tell life's
precious little golden thread
that I love it. That's
all I want.

We've got the ball of
string, the reel of packaging
tape and the optic fibre cable
but I'm sorry, we don't have
the golden thread any more.

THE FENG SHUI CONSULTANT DELIVERS HIS REPORT:—

Now that you've considered
everything — tell me where
the energies are all wrong
in my life.

Well firstly — your hair is
pointed in the wrong direction —
it should be brushed FORWARD.

Yes, Yes — and
my house? Tell
me about the
alignment of
energies in
my house.

House, doors
windows all
perfectly aligned.
Much good energy
in house.
HOWEVER.....

And the energy in your trousers is **very bad.** Car keys and wallet must <u>NEVER</u> be carried in left hand pocket in your situation

Yes, Yes.

.... neighbourhood all out of whack. Neighbourhood, city, nation and entire culture all in seriously unfortunate placement. <u>BIG TROUBLE UP AHEAD!</u> But very nice house.

Now your posture is all wrong — bad energy flow Head pointing too much downward

Leunig

Late last night when all was dark
I thought I heard a moron bark
And as the sound began to die
I heard another one reply

And then the sound became a din
As more and more morons joined in
And suddenly I realised
That they were getting organised

My blood ran cold, my skin turned grey
Remembering election day
Was not so terribly remote
And morons had the right to vote!

Australia has some nasty things
The crocodile, the fish that stings,
The snake, the spider and the shark
But worst of all, the moron's bark!

Leunig

Little, tiny, precious vote;
Underneath my overcoat,
Snug and warm against my heart,
You and me will have to part.
POLLING BOOTH
I must cast you to the horde
With your little wooden sword.
And your hopeful marching song.
Little vote of mine be strong.
Should our happy cause be dashed
And your wooden sword be smashed;
Come back dear, beloved vote;
Dream inside my overcoat.
Leunig

MATESHIP

Mateship can be very queer;
Like when a man is having strife;
A mate comes round to have a beer.
And ends up best mates with his wife!

Mateship's not all beers and skittle
Nothing really aggravates
Like those teeny, weeny, little
Devils lurking in your mates.

Leunig

DAFFODILS

I wandered lonely as a cloud
That floats on high o'er vales and hills
When all at once I saw a crowd,
Not a bit like daffodils;
Beside the lake, beneath the trees,
Politicians, if you please!

Not any likeness, could I say,
They bore to flowers, that welcome spring
Their clothes were blue and charcoal grey;
It was a most depressing thing;
So off I wandered through the hills
In search of golden daffodils.

Leunig

It was the night before
christmas and the angel
who should have been singing
in the heavens was too
weary to fly and too
depressed to sing. 🌙

☆

Sadly and aimlessly he
wandered the city streets
feeling lonelier and
lonelier as his wings
grew dirtier and more
tattered on the pavement.

He passed a mirror in a
shop and was shocked to
see how haggard and
deranged he looked —
how corrupted and
miserable.

"for a small sum I can ease your pain" spoke a voice from a doorway and soon a syringe had entered his wing and he lay down in an alley and slept.

And as the traffic roared about him the angel dreamed of his childhood — and of something even more distant and more beautiful and mysterious.

Until at last, still sleeping, he rose free from the city of pain, and returned to where he truly belonged — to the manger and the animals and to all his friends — singing their hearts out.

Leunig

How may a man
measure his own
happiness ?

He must first go
to his cupboard and
take out all his
neckties.

Then he must
lay them out on
the ground, end
to end.

Then he must measure
the length of this
line of neckties.

And that measurement;
that distance is
exactly the same ...

..... as his distance
from true happiness.

leunig

ARTIST, LEAVE THE WORLD OF ART!

Artist leave the World of Art!
Pack your goodies on a cart
Duck out through some tiny hole
And slip away and save your soul!

Leave no footprints, don't look back!
Take the dark and dirty track,
Cross the border, bless your heart;
Freedom from the World of Art!

Leunig

...it's so <u>mad</u>. How does it all hold together?

Not all of it does <u>hold</u> together. Only about a third of it holds together.

Then why doesn't it all fall apart?

Because the little bit of it that holds together is just enough to keep it all from falling apart.

See the groovy architects; what a busy bunch,
Planning public buildings while they're having lunch;
Menu on an angle, wine list on a lean;

Matchbox on a pack of smokes; what a nifty scene,—
Then the waiter cops a blast, (wine has come too early)
"Get that corkscrew out of sight — the bloody thing's too curly!"

Leunig

What the PUNTERS say about CAFÉ TWADDLE. 17 DANK PLACE, ST. KILDA

THE PUNTERS   Di Quick, designer of Albert Park, dined
with friends from work; Sheryl Van Bonk and
Lisa Lowe-Rumble.

THE OCCASION   We'd been tramping the streets all night
looking for some place to get Lisa drunk because
she wants to end it all and CAFÉ TWADDLE was the
only place with a free table

THE CONVERSATION   I didn't talk much because I was
exhausted and had a headache. Lisa was crying
most of the time and Sheryl had an argument
with the waiter who was a prize peanut.

WHAT WAS TRIED   Lisa had four fluffy ducks and locked
herself in the toilet   Sheryl and me had a piece
of black forest cake to share and some Benson and Hedges.

AND TO DRINK? I had two rocket fuels and Sheryl had the Mornington peninsula pinot noir.

THE BILL: $ 73.50 plus the cost of the toilet door.

THE VERDICT If Lisa wants to end it all, that's o.k. with me and Sheryl

SHOPPING PROVERBS

- Better to have shopped and lost than never to have shopped at all
- SHOPS WILL BE SHOPS • Shopping is the best form of defence.
- FOOLS RUSH IN WHERE ANGELS FEAR TO SHOP • The leopard does not change his shops. • WHEN THE CAT'S AWAY THE MICE WILL SHOP • Shopping is the infinite capacity to take pains.
- ANY SHOP IN A STORM • There is always room at the shop.
- SHOPPING MEN TELL NO TALES • Shopping is stranger than fiction • HELL HATH NO FURY LIKE A WOMAN SHOPPING.
- The husband is always lost to shop • TO SHOP IS HUMAN.
- Shop and the world shops with you, weep and you weep alone.
- THE CUSTOMER IS ALWAYS SHOPPING • Whom the gods would destroy they first send shopping. • WHEN THE GOING GETS TOUGH THE TOUGH GO SHOPPING • He who hesitates is shopping.
- SHOP AND LET SHOP • A little shop is a dangerous thing.
- SHOP AND YE SHALL FIND. • Empty shops make the most sound.
- YOU CANNOT RUN WITH THE HARES AND SHOP WITH THE HOUNDS.

Leunig

The FOODCOCK.

On the armchair, a
book: "HOW TO RELAX"

Beside the bed, a book;
"HOW TO GET TO SLEEP"

Next to the man,
a book; "HOW TO BE
A MAN"

Next to the window, a book; "HOW TO SEE WHAT's IN FRONT OF YOU"

On the desk, a book: "HOW TO SUCCEED IN LIFE"

In hell, a book; "HOW YOU ENDED UP IN HELL"

Leunig

The poppy pod is cut
and seeps.
The tiny child is crushed
and weeps.

The child is crushed
and crushed again
To make a special kind
of pain.

An agony which cannot
weep
But tries to rock
itself to sleep.

The poppy's weeping
does become
A special kind
of opium.

Then the child will
pluck the flower;
Each the other to
devour.

Asleep together in
the wild;
This poppy and this
little child.

Leunig

Using the time he saved by driving home on the new tollway...

... he set about making a beautiful quilt.

But suddenly,
out of nowhere...

..... he got QUILT RAGE!

Humans make you sick:
What they get up to
And what they go on about....
There's got to be some trick...

...In learning how to shrug
Instead of feeling queasy.
For me it's not so easy;
You can't educate a mug!

I get all woozy, I get sick
Like I'm peering off the edge
of paradise
I see how far the fall is
I see what makes them tick.

Yes; it's true; I'm a mug; I know.
Just looking at them : the humans.
Their frightening depth;
I'm a mug; I get vertigo.

And the way they breed
like rabbits;
Their lifestyles and their wars
Their hot pursuits and their
disgusting personal habits.

Yes, o.k., I'm a mug, I failed
to cope.
I'm some low form of stuck up
misanthrope.
It's really me that makes me ill
I should accept the way life is;
but still....
I'll repeat it short and quick;
Humans make you sick.

Leunig

I wonder,
Will it all click into place?
I feel it might.
I had a glimpse
That things could all
Come right.

I'd wake up
On a sunny, slightly roostered
morn.
And wouldn't realise at first;
The rightness would take time
To dawn.

The penny would just drop
Into my hand —
The penny that I'd lost
So long ago —
And all the peace
Withheld and blocked from me
Would start to flow.

And gradually
The thing would start to gleam;
This worried life I'd had;
This awful world;
This painful mess;
It was, in fact,
A kind of dream!

The gentle hum;
The gold and silver light
Would all resume:
The fairies and the pixies,
The particles of dust
Caught in the sunlight
In my room.

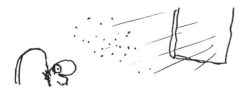

I'd pick up
Where I had been so rudely
Interrupted;
I'd have it back again for keeps:
My dog, my brilliant grasp of life,
My backyard and my paddocks
Full of time
The world all glad around me
My rightful place —
My joyous leaps.

Leunig

Is there in this life a nook
Not described in some damned book;
Or in the heart a little bird
Not yet captured by a word ;
Or in the soul a tiny breath
Which hasn't been described to death —
Something lovelier and lighter
Than the craft of some damned writer ?

Robin Hood, Robin Hood,
You'd be napalmed in the wood,
I am very sad to say,
If you were alive today

WHAT IS THIS LIFE?

LIFE IS A HOLIDAY
ON EARTH.

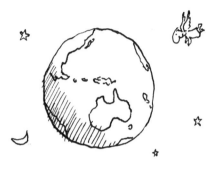

You arrive at your holiday destination and there, to meet you, wearing a big smile, is your host and guide.

HELLO, I'M YOUR MUM; I'LL GET YOU STARTED AND SHOW YOU AROUND. WOULD YOU LIKE SOME MILK?

YOU STUDY SOME MAPS, GO FOR A BIT OF AN EXPLORE AND SOON YOU'RE GETTING THE HANG OF IT. THE PLACE IS FULL OF HOLIDAY MAKERS AND BEFORE TOO LONG YOU'RE HAVING A HOLIDAY ROMANCE! AND WHY NOT?!

The accommodation is a bit unusual but it's clean and comfortable — it's your body; quite a good base for an existence

LIFE IS AN INTERESTING PLACE TO VISIT; QUITE ENJOYABLE AND WELL WORTH THE EXPERIENCE BUT YOU WOULDN'T WANT TO BE THERE TOO LONG. YOU WOULD ALWAYS FEEL LIKE A BIT OF AN OUTSIDER

HOLIDAYS ON EARTH CAN BE WONDERFUL AND HORRIBLE, BUT REGARDLESS, IT'S ALWAYS A BIT SAD WHEN THEY COME TO AN END. AND ALWAYS A GOOD FEELING TO KNOW THAT YOU'RE RETURNING HOME TO WHERE YOU REALLY BELONG; ALL REFRESHED AND WITH SOME LOVELY HOLIDAY MEMORIES.

Leunig

MUSHROOMS

Mushrooms are amazing folk;
Up into the world they poke;
Clean and tender, bold and pert
Magic from the autumn dirt.

Mushrooms, I can feel for you;
All your work of pushing through;
Pushing through the heavy dirt;
Clean and tender, bold and pert.

Leunig

YOU CAN RELY ON IT; THIS little group — this **HOUSEHOLD** is 100% **SANE**.

The woman is 40% SANE

The man is 30% SANE

making a collective, working sanity of exactly 100% (OPTIMUM)

The hound is
30% SANE....

If one of the group has an
"episode", causing, for example,
a 10% loss of sanity, the
remaining two will set
about making up the shortfall

By a supreme effort of
will, discipline and concentration
the remaining two will each
generate an extra 5% sanity.
The problem is that the effort
involved may cause the eyes to
bulge in such a manner that the
entire situation looks TOTALLY MAD.

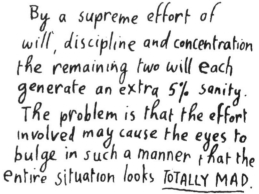

Leunig

Look at your socks
on the floor!
WHAT AN INTERNATIONAL
DISGRACE!

Yeah, well look at your
new haircut. What an
international joke. Talk about
ruining our overseas reputation!

O.K. then! What do you
imagine Robert Hughes
would say about the porcelain
pussy cat you've just purchased
for the mantelpiece?
How
embarrassing!

What about your dorky, saggy
underpants. What would Germaine
Greer say about those? She'd
laugh her head off!

What about the peanut bowl
you made on your stupid
wood lathe. What would
Barry Humphries or Clive
　　　　　James say
　　　about that?

What would you
Say if I called
you a sexy, juicy
woman?

I'd call you
a hot, wild
beast!

Leunig

Children who will not leave home

Children who will not leave home are becoming a big problem!

Sometimes they get into the ceiling and build nests and cannot be flushed out or dislodged.

They travel along power lines
at night and visit nests of
neighbouring children in the
roofs of other houses.....

Where they mate and fight
and cause a terrible din.
A nest of grandchildren in
the roof is a particularly
nasty situation and is certainly
a major headache.

Leunig

OUR LIFE IN BIZARRE, SECRET CULT.

We are married. We are known as "husband" and "wife". We don't refer to each other as "my partner"

We are not "guys" We don't answer to, "Hey guys!" Sometimes we answer to "Hello folks"

We love going to bed early — sometimes with a piece of fruit to eat. A good sleep is one of our greatest pleasures.

On the odd occasion we have
sardines on toast for breakfast
on saturday morning — with
a dash of vinegar, a pinch of
salt and a bit of pepper. These
are the important little details.

We do not talk to computers
We CANNOT talk to computers.
We CAN talk to dogs and cats.
— and we do! Quite a lot if
the truth be known.
We have no knowledge of
"The Simpsons" whatsoever —
which is a lovely feeling and a
rare privilege.

We consistently avoid sausage
sizzles, garage sales, gymnasiums
television sets and cinemas.
So there you have it. This
is our bizarre secret cult.

leunig

THE SHADOW MINISTER FOR JOY.

The Shadow Minister for Joy
Got up to make his maiden speech
Soup stains on his corduroy
And munching on a juicy peach
Lipstick marks around his neck
A yellow rose upon his vest
He laughed and said, "Well what the heck!
We wish him all the very best.

Leunig

Little Tendrils

Little tendrils of the heart
Curling out and groping,
Seeking little things to hold,
Wiggling and hoping.

Little tendrils of the soul,
Delicate and perky
Seeking little surfaces,
Peculiar and quirky

Little tendrils, little tendrils,
Innocent and plucky,
I pray that you are careful
And I hope that you are lucky.

The only thing worth being in this life, is a simpleton.

Yes but _how_ ??

THERE IS NO NETWORK! NO CLUB!

THERE IS NO MAGAZINE !

NO COURSE !
NO DIPLOMA !

You have to go it alone !

Leunig

Life is but a leap into a bucket;
Seize a juicy saveloy and suck it
Tell your enemies to go and shove it;
Plunge into your life and try to love it

Leunig